MODERN GUIDE FOR NEW PARENTS:

Best advice for new parents

Clinton M.Wellman

Table of contents

Chapter one

Your Parenting Style

We as a whole need to be the best guardians we can be for our kids, yet there is as often as possible going against guidance on the most proficient method to raise a youth that is certain, kind, and effective. Furthermore, all aspects of being a parent have been more troublesome and tenser during the pestilence, with guardians shuffling complex new obligations and unpleasant new decisions, all while managing the customary inquiries that surface in regular daily existence with the youngsters we love. All through the carnival demonstration of nurturing, it's essential to focus on adjusting needs, shuffling commitments, and quick exchanging between the requests of your kids, other relatives, and yourself. Current guardians have the entire web available to them and follow no one power. It's difficult to tell whom or what to trust. Here, we'll talk about how to help your child to grow up to be an individual you really appreciate without losing yourself simultaneously. You believe your adolescent should tune in, regard, and trust you as opposed to fear you. You need to be a useful, yet not floating, overly controlling guardian.

These things are easy to lay out as targets, however difficult to achieve. How would you track down the fitting equilibrium?

As your child develops, the obstructions might modify, and your considerations might move, yet your methodology ought to be consistent, extreme, and mindful. Assist your adolescent with understanding by means of involvement that trying makes certainty and assists you with figuring out how to oversee impediments. Adjust your assumptions regarding what your child is equipped for achieving freely, whether you have a child figuring out how to stay asleep for the entire evening, a baby helping to put toys away, or a more established kid addressing issues.

Keep in mind, there is no legitimate technique to bring up a youngster. Give your all, trust yourself and partake in the organization of the little individual in your life.

Actual discipline, like beating and hitting, will in general make forceful conduct in youths. Remember that it's generally a parental triumph in the event that you can approach a situation to such an extent that a youngster is procuring freedoms (screentime, for instance) by appropriate conduct, as opposed to losing them as an outcome. Look for charming activities to acclaim and reward, and small kids will need to recreate the experience. However, inescapably, parenthood involves a specific number of "terrible cop" minutes, when you need to say no or end and your child will be enraged at you — and that is perfect, it goes with the domain. Search in the mirror and work on getting out whatever guardians have consistently said: "I'm your mom/father, I'm not your companion."

As guardians, we ought to look to control our kids' lead — or to help them to direct their own — and making an effort not to oversee their considerations: \Self-guideline is the ability to fathom and deal with your way of behaving and your reactions to feelings and things happening around you.

It includes having the option to:

control reactions to extraordinary feelings including irritation, excitement, fury, and embarrassment
quiet down after something exciting or upsetting\focus on a task\refocus consideration on a new task\control impulses\behave in manners that assist you with coexisting with others.
Why self-guideline is urgent

As your child creates, self-guideline helps them:

learn at school - in light of the fact that self-guideline gives your child the ability to sit and tune in the classroom\behave in socially OK ways - on the grounds that self-guideline enables your youngster to oversee driving forces
make companions - on the grounds that self-guideline enables your kid to alternate in games and discussion, share toys, and express feelings in suitable ways\become more free - on the grounds that self-guideline empowers your kid to arrive at fitting conclusions about conduct and figure out how to act in new circumstances with less direction from you.
How and when self-guideline creates
Kids learn self-guideline through warm and responsive associations. They additionally foster it by watching the grown-ups around them.

Self-guideline starts when youngsters are infants. It fills chiefly in the baby and preschool years, yet it additionally keeps up with developing straight into adulthood.

For instance, babies could suck their fingers for solace or turn away from their carers in the event that they need a break from consideration or are feeling exhausted.

Little children might hang tight for brief lengths for food and toys. Be that as it may, babies may as yet take things from different kids assuming that it's something they really want. Also, fits of rage happen when children are overpowered by extraordinary feelings.

Preschoolers are figuring out how to know how to play with different kids and handle what's generally anticipated of them. For instance, a preschooler might endeavor to talk in a delicate voice in the event that you're at the films.

Young youths are developing better at managing their longings and requirements, imagining others' perspectives, and seeing all sides of an issue. This infers, for instance, that they might contradict different adolescents without belligerence.

Youngsters and youths are better at arranging, remaining with extreme exercises, acting in socially adequate ways, and examining what their activities mean for others. For instance, your high school youngster could consider your perspective while they're wheeling and dealing with you over their time limitation.

Chapter two

BE A GOOD ROLE MODEL

Each parent ought to be a good example to their child. Your child is continually seeing what you do; he/she sees how you deal with your feelings, stress, reactions, and connections, especially with others. While it is in your space to raise, supply, and sustain your child, it is likewise important to persistently set a guide to impersonate, which is a foundation to fostering a healthy kid.

Being a decent good example might be extreme since your child will observe the most obviously terrible pieces of you; they see you adapt to life difficulties, and see you when you have fizzled and at your lowest times. While babies retain the great and the horrible sides of what happens around them, these rules will help them filter through and structure their schedules.

The first is to promise you are anxious for personal development; this ought to continually be in our viewpoints. Guarantee you investigate new encounters and extend your perspectives, this won't teach our kids to ever quit creating since there's continuously a new thing to learn in this world. Attempt to discover some new information consistently.

Participate in solid living by eating suitably and practicing much of the time. This won't just upgrade your life yet in addition set a model for your adolescent. While this is indispensable to stay away from kid weight, which could prompt bitterness and affliction, guardians ought to likewise not overdo it since balance is vital. The accentuation ought to be on a solid way of life.

Make it a normal practice to serve and chip in, especially as a family. It is a phenomenal method to advance family fellowship, and joint effort abilities and develop a youth with a giving heart. Continually urge your child to carry the necessities of others into the brain and give some assistance when required.

All the more significantly, carry on with an open life and don't disguise your identity as an individual to your child. Share your related involvements with the two blunders and accomplishments, when pertinent. Show him that weakness is a goodness that comes from a position of force. Take your adolescent to work with you and let them witness your everyday practice. Status doesn't make any difference, yet your disposition and your personality mean the world. This is additionally pertinent to your poise. How you approach communicating feelings before your child has its suggestions, either advantageous or destructive. As extreme as it very well may be, practicing poise however much as could be expected before your kid is vital. Stay quiet and deal with that fierceness. In the event that need be, take it out at the exercise center or go for a long run.

Assemble the right associations, since it is essential. Not all connections might be wonderful especially among more distant family individuals since there may be clashes starting from your kin, sisters, guardians, or parents in law, be the middle person and mean to keep a cheerful association with everybody. Make it as hard as workable for anyone to say anything horrendous about you. Be a starter and consistently acknowledge moral obligation first.

Continuously being polite and giving a listening ear, this shows young people how to be sure by recognizing what their identity is and paying attention to their own extraordinary conclusions. This is a difficult part of initiative, however the best chiefs listen intently and say essentially less. Open your brain and your ears to everything your kids are saying to you. They will, thus, figure out how to do a similar sometime down the road.

In particular, as guardians, you ought to continuously talk about what you intend what you say. Allow your words to be upheld by genuine activity. Be a father who remains by his proclamations as it raises your worth and worth.
Mother and little girl both wear shades. Mother tells the best way to be a decent parent by Improving nurturing skills, nurturing guidance
Walk the walk. Try not to just let your child know what you believe they should do.
The best way to deal with instructing is to show them.
Human is an unmistakable animal categories to a limited extent since we can learn through impersonation 1 . We are wired to duplicate others' demonstrations,

decipher them, and acclimatize them into our own. Youngsters, specifically, notice all that their folks do very eagerly. There is no such thing as cherishing your child to an extreme. Adoring them can't indulge them 2
.
Your kids and teens are consistently seeing what you do. They notice how you oversee pressure. They screen how you treat others and notice how you adapt to your feelings. They retain up all that information like minuscule wipes. In any event, when you accept your kids aren't focusing, it's critical to be a decent good example.

Social Learning Theory
As indicated by the social learning speculation, people advance by noticing others.
1 For example, the exemplary Bobo doll explore showed how children duplicate grown-up conduct. Scientists saw that youths took care of a doll the same way the grown-ups did.

Youngsters who saw a grown-up become unfriendly with the doll were forceful in their connections also. In the interim, young people who saw grown-ups treat the doll energetically mirrored the liberality.

You most likely needn't bother with a refined logical examination to see that children duplicate their folks. You without a doubt notice it consistently.

While you're clearing the floor, you could see your little one professing to clear as well. Or on the other hand, you could hear your preschooler put her rich bear to sleep the same way you fold her up around evening time. Kids rehash what they hear, and they duplicate what they see. Thus, you should watch out for the things you're accidentally showing your child.

Your kids and teens are constantly seeing what you do. They notice how you oversee pressure. They screen how you treat others and notice how you adapt to your feelings. They assimilate up all that information like little wipes. In any event, when you accept your kids aren't focusing, it's pivotal to be a decent good example.

Social Learning Theory

As per the social learning speculation, people advance by noticing others.

1 For example, the exemplary Bobo doll analyze represented how children duplicate grown-up conduct. Scientists saw that young people dealt with a doll the same way the grown-ups did.

Youngsters who saw a grown-up become unfriendly with the doll were forceful in their connections too. In the mean time, adolescents who saw grown-ups treat the doll energetically imitated the liberality.

You presumably needn't bother with a modern logical examination to see that children duplicate their folks. You without a doubt notice it consistently.

While you're clearing the floor, you could see your little one professing to clear as well. Or on the other hand, you could hear your preschooler put her extravagant bear to sleep the same way you fold her up around evening time. Kids rehash what they hear, and they duplicate what they see. Hence, you should watch out for the things you're unconsciously showing your child.

What Behavior Are You Modeling?
Now and again, you could accidentally impersonate hurtful propensities for your children. Think about these potential outcomes.

A woman tells the clerk at an eatery that her kid is just 11 so she might get a rebate at the smorgasbord. Her child learns it's OK to lie every so often to accomplish what you need.

A dad gos through his evenings staring at the TV, however tells his 14-year-old little girl she ought to understand more.

Guardians train their children to approach everybody with deference. However, they routinely offer negative comments about others behind their backs.

A separated two or three debates continually care issues and visits, yet they believe that their children should coexist with each other.

A parent advises her child to quit placing his fingers in his mouth; yet when she's apprehensive, she nibbles her fingernails.

A mother urges her girl to be courteous to other people, yet she yells at the shop representative when the business won't acknowledge back a thing she wishes to return.

A dad lets his children know that they ought to eat appropriately, yet he takes dessert after they hit the sack.

Guardians help their children to share and be caring with what they have, yet they never make gifts or become taken part in any type of noble cause or volunteer movement.

A dad smokes cigarettes. While he grasps a cigarette, he cautions his children that smoking is terrible and that they ought to never take up the propensity.

Guardians ask their children to acknowledge liability regarding their activities and their choices. However, when guardians disregard their kid's dental arrangement, they fight with the secretary and tell her she unquestionably committed a booking error.

The most effective method to Teach Kids Anger Management Skills

Adhere to Your Own Guidelines

It's unbelievably difficult to show adequate direct for your children constantly, and nobody is anticipating that you should be perfect. Be that as it may, you ought to attempt to demonstrate the principles and propensities you believe that your children should follow.

For example, on the off chance that you don't believe that your children should be harassed, it's most likely just plain dumb for you to keep utilizing e-cigarettes. Moreover, assuming you maintain that your children should be valid, you ought to expect frankly. For instance, assuming you utter harmless exaggerations as opposed to tell the truth, your children will discover that lying is OK.

Tell your children the best way to submit to your family rules by showing them each time you have.

2 Likewise, apply discipline that shows fundamental abilities and make sense of how these guidelines will help them further down the road. Assuming you show to young people that you submit to the guidelines, it will help the adequacy of your disciplinary strategies.

There might be circumstances when you want to explain any decisions that can confuse.

For example, on the off chance that your pal heats you a cake, and you think it tastes terrible, you actually may let them know saving their emotions was phenomenal. When any such thing happens, you'll need to clear up for your kids that you would have rather not hurt your companion's feelings.

Model Life Skills

You likewise have the open door consistently to carry on with a day to day existence worth mimicking. Ponder what you maintain that your children should gain from you and endeavor to repeat it in your life. Normally, there might be events when you make mistakes or don't get things done exactly as you had planned. Yet, that is OK.

Chapter three

PRACTICE KIND AND FIRM POSITIVE PARENTING

Positive nurturing and positive discipline accentuate showing acceptable conduct by means of sympathetic and thorough parental strategies. Here are some stupendous positive nurturing strategies to assist you with fostering a quiet, upbeat family.

What Is Positive Parenting?

Positive nurturing is a nurturing technique that contends youngsters are conceived great and with the longing to make the best choice. It underlines the requirement for common regard and embracing useful procedures to rebuff. The positive nurturing techniques center around showing the great future way of behaving rather than rebuffing late wrongdoing.

During the 1920s, Viennese specialists, Alfred Adler and Rudolf Dreikurs were acquainted with the United States' positive nurturing strategies1. Nurturing specialists and associations across the world have consequently made and supported a few decent nurturing rehearses.

Numerous advanced guardians embrace these delicate nurturing rehearses in light of the fact that they don't want to parent how they were educated.

Positive nurturing demonstrates guardians might bring cheerful youngsters up in manners that mirror their family values and points of view. Positive guardians are open to their kids' requirements, formative stages, and personality. Among the four Baumrind nurturing styles, positive nurturing is a legitimate nurturing style.

mother father girl embrace family social affairs positive nurturing
Advantages Of Positive Parenting
Fewer BEHAVIOR PROBLEMS

Many studies have demonstrated that positive discipline conveys favorable results regarding the kid's lead and close-to-home development.
Conversely, cruel, reformatory nurturing in youth will in general bring about higher conduct problems. Guardians who are crisp, uninvolved, and negligent produce mess around with lower self-guideline, which further fuels the kid's conduct troubles.

CLOSE PARENT-CHILD RELATIONSHIP
A decent parent doesn't have to reprimand their youngster to correct an undesirable way of behaving. There is no really shouting, epic showdown, or enmity. Subsequently, the parent-kid elements change, and their bond gets to the next level.

Besides, shared regard and genuine correspondence increment the parent-youngster relationship.

mother and girl watch iPad together rehearsing positive.

nurturing

BETTER SELF-ESTEEM AND MENTAL WELL-BEING

Youngsters supported with great nurturing have better confidence. They believe they can accomplish undertakings as successfully as most different kids.

These kids are additionally stronger. They return quickly from difficulties.

Kids who are versatile with fearlessness have less family struggle and better bonds with their caring guardians. They will more often than not have more grounded mental health.

More noteworthy SCHOOL PERFORMANCE

Decidedly nurtured kids partake in the better scholarly achievement. A more grounded parent-youngster tie beginning from this nurturing approach is likewise extensively associated with scholarly achievement.

mother little girl concentrates on before a PC applying fitting nurturing practices and positive nurturing

BETTER SOCIAL COMPETENCE

Kids with positive guardians have the more prominent social critical thinking skill and social self-viability. They are all the more composed and have a strong identity.

Really PARENTING SELF-ESTEEM AND LESS STRESS

Kids are not by any means the only ones who benefit from powerful nurturing. Analysts have found that guardians who practice powerful nurturing additionally help confidence and trust in their nurturing. They experience less nurturing-related pressure as the kids have self-control and are polite.

Positive Parenting Tips\s1. Center Around THE REASONS BEHIND THE BEHAVIORS There is dependably a justification for why youngsters act mischievously, despite the fact that the reasons might look senseless to the guardians.

It is sensible for the youngster, and that is the reason they act that way.

In the event that guardians can address the reason speedily, regardless of whether the adolescent gets the preciseness exact thing they need, they would, in any case, feel that their requirements are perceived. Having basic encouragement from the family is normally more fundamental than having the real wish accomplished.

A revered youngster might go on without the prerequisite to make trouble. They might in any case feel aggravated, yet they don't have to carry on to be seen.

Ask them inquiries and get to the wellspring of the matter. Utilizing undivided attention and knowing the purpose for the hazardous ways of behaving may likewise assist guardians with keeping away from them in any case.

For instance, a youngster hit her sister. The explanation might be that she was irritated when her little sibling took her toy. So training the more youthful adolescent to request consent first prior to swiping another person's things could prevent what is going on from happening. Doing it is additionally showing youths incredible habits.

A young lady questions a child sibling over the stacked toy. With valuable discipline, nobody refuses to accept responsibility for the issues at hand positive nurturing

On the off chance that your young person appears to never pay attention to you, there are two primary clarifications.

One element might be your assumption is ridiculous. Reevaluate what you request that your adolescent do or not do. Is that an order or a solicitation? Does it have a genuine explanation?

It's more straightforward for a youngster to acknowledge a decent clarification, explicitly one that is fundamental to their prosperity than to follow a request indiscriminately.

One more element of defiance is an absence of a nearby parent-kid relationship, which makes the foundation for a youngster's development, mental health, and future achievement.

2. BE KIND AND FIRM

Be delicate with your adolescent to tell the best way to be quite conscious to other people.

Kids advance by duplicating others, and you are their key good example.

At the point when a parent yells, embarrasses, or calls kid names, the youth figures out how to do the equivalent when they're disappointed.

The opposite is likewise obvious. At the point when a parent is overall quite gracious regardless of being insulted, the young person figures out how to deal with circumstances with quiet and deference.

Being respectful likewise assists a youngster with quieting down, being available to reasoning, and being more anxious to collaborate.

Being sympathetic isn't equivalent to surrender.

Many guardians wrongly interface being well-mannered and friendly with being permissive.

This isn't accurate.

You ought to in any case make impediments, and yet, you implement them pleasantly and powerfully. For instance, you may immovably and mercifully prompt a youngster that she can't have what she wants. There is compelling reason need to holler, expect a foul tone, or talk firmly. A harsh voice communicates wrath through a strong voice shows power.

You needn't bother with being unsavory to mean business. A strong and calm NO is essentially as great as, while possibly worse than, a boisterous and terrible NO.

You might be harsh in characterizing cutoff points and executing sanctions with the goal that your young person realizes what's in store and what to put together their future choices with respect to.

Rehearsing dynamic this strategy assists youngsters with reinforcing their mental reasoning, a basic ability for their future achievement.

3. Delicate DISCIPLINE
As per Jane Nelsen in Positive Discipline: The First Three Years, reformatory discipline energizes Four Rs that don't help a youngster's development - Resentment, Rebellion, Revenge, and Retreat.

Frequently, invented adverse results can't deter shocking acts, nor might they at any point show useful ones.

At the point when guardians holler or reprove, they make a horrible pattern of impulse. The coercive cycle has been exhibited to add to social issues and direct challenges, for example, oppositional disobedient confusion in kids.

A charming, non-corrective response is fundamentally more fruitful in relieving an overwhelmed youth and connecting with them to get familiar with another movement.

The break has been cruelly scrutinized lately. That is on the grounds that most guardians don't utilize it correctly7.

Opportunity for youngsters shouldn't be a discipline however unfortunately, most guardians use it that way. They isolated and limit the adolescent's development and add an additional discipline by berating or reproving the youngster.

In the first idea of a break, the young person is just taken out from the over-invigorating climate that makes or bothers rowdiness, and afterward put into a non-supporting space to quiet down and feel great.

So some nurturing specialists made "time-in" to supplant break. Time-in is on a very basic level a comparable plan to the right usage of break, which has been demonstrated to manage many years of exploration by clinicians.

Utilizing breaks isn't the solitary way to deal with decreasing unsavory behavior. Positive Discipline A-Z: 1001 Ideas to Everyday Parenting Problems, likewise by Nelsen, is loaded with fantastic guidance, replies, and suggestions on powerful discipline.

Be that as it may, it is difficult to recall every one of the 1001 responses or consistently have the book prepared when you really want it. So it's pivotal to be innovative and adaptable while rebuffing.

Keep in mind that a positive nurturing approach centers around showing the proper way of behaving instead of rebuffing the undesirable ones.

4. BE CLEAR AND BE CONSISTENT
Choose and make sense of the punishments of penetrating guidelines plainly prior to being implemented. What's more, guardians should be steady and completely finish them.

In the event that a parent isn't predictable, there will be disarray.

The kid might keep up with pushing or squeezing the limitations to find what else may occur.

To finish demonstrate say nothing except if you would not joke about this.

Try not to convey misleading intimidations to drop the ball game assuming your child acts up except if you are ready to follow it through when that works out.

5. AGE-APPROPRIATE BEHAVIOR AND BRAIN DEVELOPMENT

In some cases, what we see as unsatisfactory lead is an age-fitting way of behaving.

For example, fits of rage among little children are very regular. These youthful little children have enormous feelings yet can't communicate them in words. They likewise don't have the ability to oversee themselves since that part of the mind isn't yet framed. Our baby needs our direction in figuring out how to control it.

Phases of mental health have importance in picking a decent nurturing method. Babies and preschoolers (even three-year-olds) may not appreciate the ramify.

Chapter four

BE A SAFE HAVEN FOR YOUR CHILD

Tell your child that you'll constantly show up for them by being open to your kid's signs and delicate to their requirements. Backing and embracing your child as a person. Be a warm and agreeable area for your child to investigate and get back to.

Youngsters raised by guardians who are continually responsive prone to have better profound guideline improvement, interactive abilities advancement, and emotional wellness results.

Home, which recently filled in as our shelter, is presently not a safe haven for the vast majority of us. We get back to a blast of mail, bills, phone messages, and obligations. PDAs and email connect us constantly with the rest of the world, simultaneously upsetting our touch with our loved ones. In certain houses, the TV is on ceaselessly, shooting fresh insight about unfortunate events and life and demise circumstances.

To develop, we as a whole need a safe climate — both truly and genuinely — to return home to. In the event that kids are to give total consideration to the different requests of growing up, they need a steady, strong family where they feel safeguarded. They need to accept we can guard kids: from the neighborhood menace, from ruffians, from psychological militants.

What's more, regardless of how independent they are as they seek after their side interests outside the house, kids need to realize they can depend on the presence of their folks when they get back. Your kids would like to be with you than do anything more on the planet for quite a while. In any event, when children begin having sleepovers and long-distance race ball games, when they return home they need two things: a safe shelter where they can be absolutely themselves, and associate with the remainder of the family in a profound, agreeable, and euphoric way. Assuming your youth seems to live principally for screen time, she's displaying a more profound need that necessities fulfilling.

Giving your kids a shelter is an incredible gift. It empowers them to go out and battle the conflict on the planet, then returns home to re-energize. It likewise offers your family culture the agreeable home it needs to prosper. At last, research recommends that people who effectively configure homes where they find nurturance and excellence report further developed temperaments and less unpleasant lives.

So what can really be done, in this rushed world, to lay out a shelter for your loved ones?

1. Dial back.

We as whole love energy, yet stress kills. In a real sense. Stress dissolves our understanding, our capacity to do everything we can for our children, and our well-being. To be fair, we can ordinarily perceive how we make our lives more upsetting than they should be, essentially by being reluctant to pursue the decision to dial back. In the event that you believe your children should act better, begin by dialing back and not hurrying to such an extent.

2. Your kids' house is their safe haven.
That implies all home individuals treat each other appropriately, and no brutality, physical or verbal, is permitted, particularly among youngsters. Click here for tips on the best way to prevent your children from battling with one another.

3. Make an effort not to over-structure time at home.
Home should be low-pressure time, not execution time. Obviously, all kids should be useful individuals from the home. However, kids likewise need bunches of time to

unwind. Do whatever it takes not to suffocate them with an excessive number of obligations on top of homework, essential housework, music practice, strict examinations, and so forth. Young people, especially, are habitually under extraordinary pressure.

4. Acknowledge your youngsters' "Child Self."

You know the Baby Self. That piece of your child shows up in the pretense of relapse when your young person has been managing heaps of "grown-up" assumptions. The entire day they endeavor hard to maintain a reasonable level of control at school. At the point when you show there, you summon the newborn child self by simply being their parent. They go to pieces. They whimper or if nothing else act somewhat adolescent.

Would it be a good idea for you to chasten them, and request a reasonable way of behaving? Indeed, how might you feel assuming you were overpowered and whiney and your companion or companion mentioned that you act all the more maturely? All children need an opportunity to be their child self, and the more youthful they are, the additional time the child self should be "out". Assuming that you let your child be "little" when they should be (comfortable minutes, sleep time, when they are tired) you decrease the chance they'll disintegrate at unseemly times (supper with Grandma, in line at the store) (supper with Grandma, in line at the general store.)

My recommendation is to empower small kids to partake in their "Child Selves" at home when doable. You might expect fits or tears or groan following a monotonous day at preschool, after her most memorable sleepover, after the school execution she buckled down on, or basically on Friday evening following a bustling week. All young people need to strive to play out a high level of the time, from standing by at school to dealing with companions to choosing that sprinter at a respectable starting point. They all need time to let the "Child Self" arise without being taunted.

Furthermore, despite the fact that it frequently shows up as though they'll remain newborn children perpetually, their Baby Selves will go sooner than you can suspect, alongside your vehicle keys.

5. Give sufficient construction so that kids' schedules work dependably.
Kids need to know what to expect. Envision yourself sitting dealing with a venture when your significant other unexpectedly illuminates you it's the ideal opportunity for a little while with the inlaws. Kids regularly feel like they have little impact over their life; irritating that springing plan changes on them generally delivers obstruction. The construction likewise makes things more arranged, limiting the pressure of rehashed somewhat late chases after stuff. Click here

for more on creating family customs and construction.

6. Limit Technology.

Set a positive model by closing off your PC and cell phone to go through the night with your loved ones. Make it a family decide that Saturdays are without innovation. Stressed over how you'll adapt? That is a strong marker that your home necessities to anticipate a standard sans tech day. Attempt it as a trial. You could all vibe unusual when you fire scouring toward another — "Hello, you live here?" — however, the closeness will clear you away, and you won't return.

7. Be aware of the impact of sound.

One specialist I know has quieting music, or cascades, in each room of his home. He refers to different explorations demonstrating that peaceful sounds give food to the resistant framework as well as the spirit.

The furthest edge of this range, obviously, is clearly TV, troubling news, and stunning traffic.

, you might find it fascinating that seeing eye canines that live in urban communities had more limited lives because of unpleasant commotion levels. Anything you can do to restrict traffic commotions will protect your family actually and inwardly.

Chat WITH YOUR CHILD AND HELP THEIR BRAINS INTEGRATE

The majority of us definitely know the worth of correspondence. Converse with your adolescent and furthermore pay attention to them mindfully. By having an open channel of correspondence, you'll have a superior association with your child, and your young person will come to you when there's an issue.

Be that as it may, there's one more reason for correspondence. You help your child to interface different segments of their mind, a vital stage in a kid's development.

The combination is comparable to our body in which different organs need to facilitate and cooperate to support a sound body. At the point when different locales of the cerebrum are connected, they might work agreeably overall, which infers fewer fits, all the more appropriate conduct, more compassion, and worked on mental prosperity.

Chapter five

Accept all the aid you can obtain as a new parent.

Never before in history have parents and fathers been asked to care for their newborns...all alone. We always had parents, aunts, and older sisters staying with us to assist out. And when both parents work, they're much more stressed. So, my suggestion for new parents? Don't hesitate to seek or pay for assistance. You need...and deserve it. Lean on your friends and family, seek into SNOO, or get some aid. You'll get more sleep and appreciate your lovely developing family more completely.

Rely on the compassion of strangers

Need to get your 60-inch stroller through a rotating door? Can't seem to handle your vehicle keys, diaper bag, groceries, and car seat all at once? There's a time and place, particularly while out and about, to just ask for aid from a stranger.

But how do you take the plunge? "The ideal way is to make eye contact and a grin so that the individual knows you're gazing squarely at them," says Cook. "You may say, 'Hi there, my hands are so full right now, could you mind opening the door for me?' Always say thank you for their aid as people prefer to be acknowledged for their acts of kindness."

Even when you believe you've got everything covered, don't hesitate to ask for help.

Communicating our wants may be tough at any stage of life — and it doesn't get easier when a kid comes. During this time of uphill struggles — some real (like pushing a stroller up a flight of stairs) and others metaphorical (like coping with postpartum anxiety) — it's not uncommon to feel uneasy about asking for assistance.

It's only normal to feel that we're intruding on others by asking for help. But striving to get through infant care single-handedly might leave you feeling overwhelmed and alone. Parenting your new little one demands enormous levels of energy and courage, and it's great if you're not able to summon them at the time.

To assist you to obtain what you need at this time, we talked to parents and communication experts on methods to ask for — and get –meaningful aid. Here are 12 of their finest techniques for asking relatives, friends, co-workers, and even your spouse to provide help.

1. Clarify what you need

Real talk: Amidst the rigors of the motherhood transition, we're not always thinking with perfect clarity. Running on fumes and up to your ears in soiled onesies, you may feel shadowed by a foggy mist of must-dos. To gain the most beneficial support, first attempt cutting through the confusion with a basic writing assignment.

“A bullet list or notebook may be an excellent approach to suss out what’s going on in your mind,” says licensed clinical psychologist Dr. Anna Hiatt Nicholaides. “Once you have recognized your need, you can think about how to articulate it.” Make a note of everything that seems overwhelming, then organize it into groups of greatest to lowest importance.

Use a food service template... but not only for meals

Websites like Meal Train and Take Them a Meal are fantastic for scheduling home-cooked meals for family and friends. Surprisingly, their helpfulness may go beyond meatloaf and casserole.

These types of templates can schedule all sorts of services from loved ones, from chores to babysitting. You may even use them to communicate things that are hard to speak about in person. “Be careful to explain preferences on how long people may remain and visit with you, as well as information on any food restrictions or preferences,”

Outsource your requirements

Can’t bring yourself to ask your BFF to wipe the muck off your dinner plates? Now you may ask a stranger to do it. Sites like Task Rabbit allow you to search a database of persons who want nothing more than to assist you out with home jobs for a little buck. (And sure, they have to pass background checks.)

If finance permits, this sort of here-and-there aid might be your route to less stress.

Experiment with additional supporting online platforms

These days, there’s no lack of applications and websites aimed to alleviate new parents’ responsibilities. Consider letting one of them digitize your baby-related requirements.

"After delivering twins and recognizing that I needed additional assistance, I organized a signup using SignUp Genius for folks to come over and cuddle my kids and give them their bottles," explains parent Bethany C. "In addition to the physical aid, it was extremely good to receive some social connection during that chaotic time."

"One way new parents may express their needs successfully when the baby comes is by utilizing Trello boards as to-do lists," says marital and family therapist Katie Ziskind, LMFT. Trello's digital organizing tools are commonly used for business cooperation – but there's no reason they can't do the same for home obligations.

Online communication may even be the finest means of remaining on the same page as your spouse, particularly if you have hectic schedules. “Create means to communicate you can both read, such as utilizing Google’s Keep,” says Ziskind.

Keep your to-do list handy

Keeping a concrete list on hand won’t simply help you go through your ideas, it’ll offer direction for others.

“When visitors come, they typically want to hold the baby for you. What you may need, however, is for somebody to cook you a meal, throw in a load of laundry, or clean the toilet,” explains private practice counselor Kayce Hodos, LPC. “Have a list of duties that seem difficult to attend to, and when others ask what you need, give it over.”

Don’t be scared to follow up

Reaching out once is hard enough. Doing it a second time might feel much more awkward. So when the buddy who said she’d clean for you doesn’t come or a dinner delivery goes missing, you may feel apprehensive about following up. Don't be, says Nicholaides.

"It is disappointing to have your needs overlooked, particularly when you're committing your life to your infant's needs, but you deserve to be cared for," she urges. "Persist in striving to satisfy your needs, whatever they may be. If your partner is unresponsive, turn to your relatives or close friends."

Try putting yourself in the other person's shoes: Wouldn't you want to know if you dropped the ball on aiding a friend?

Choose someone to delegate to you

When you feel self-conscious about reaching out, how about selecting someone who can make requests on your behalf? "I had a friend who insisted I select one of three ways she could help me, so I picked a Meal Train and it was simply the nicest thing," recounts parent Whitney S.

"My recommendation would be to go via a trusted friend or family member who can make things happen so you don't have to worry about imposing." We all have that one family member who won't hesitate to voice their thoughts. Use them!

Try a support group

For anyone with less-than-perfect relationships with family (uh, all of us) it may be easier to share burdens with those outside our immediate circle. Enter the parent support group.

These organizations may be found for every new-parent concern from nursing to babywearing. Hey, it never hurts to spend time with those in the same boat as you, right?

You also never know what useful doors a support group could open. "I attended a La Leche League meeting where I met several great ladies. That finally lead me to locate a doctor who could assist with my baby's tongue tie," recounts Bethany C.

Reach out to a professional

Lactation consultants, pediatricians, and family therapists exist for a purpose. With some post-baby difficulties, aid from friends and family can only go you so far. Perhaps it's time to get in contact with a professional.

Wondering how to locate the perfect mental health pro? "If a new mom is trying to locate a therapist who may be of assistance, go out to other new parents who presumably have used support as well," says Lauren Cook, MMFT. "Psychology Today is another fantastic resource if a new parent is confused about where to look."

For questions about baby care or feeding, don't hesitate to check in with your baby's doc. "Many physicians have lactation nurses on staff, and if they don't, they should have advice on where to turn," adds Hodos.

Don't lose your sense of humor when you become a first-time parent.
Remember, perfection is found only in the dictionary. So, forget decorum, forget organization, be patient with yourself and...laugh, laugh, laugh! Laughter lifts your spirits, decreases your tension, and is just what this doctor prescribes!
Take care of each other. And do some exciting things!
Caring for your infant is just half your work; the other is giving your main squeeze some TLC. Step out for supper or a stroll when a family member comes to visit. Find time to cook together, lounge on the sofa, and maybe even...wait for it...you know!

Chapter six

Find Kids Being Good

Have you at any point paused to ponder how often you reply badly to your youngsters on a particular day? You can wind up reprimanding more often than commending. How would you feel about a boss that treated you with so much regrettable direction, regardless of whether it was benevolent?

The most persuasive tactic is to discover youngsters ever figuring things out: "You made your bed without being asked – that is remarkable!" or "I was watching you play with your sister and you were unusually persistent." These assertions will accomplish different things to invigorate proper behavior long-term than repetitive scoldings.

Try searching down something to applaud constantly. Be generous with remunerations

– your love, hugs, and compliments can do some great things and are in many instances beyond spectacular. Before long you will notice you are "developing" a higher degree of the behavior you would desire to observe. It is crucial to inform your youngster when they have performed nicely. Offering positive consideration for the excellent manner of behaving is a fantastic technique for exhibiting to a youngster which behavior you enjoy and aid them in advance with those wonderful ways of behaving.

What You Will Need

Little incentives, akin to a most favorite snack, TV program, screen time, stickers, or a most cherished item.

What to Do

From the start, try to find your child becoming excellent randomly, or maybe one moment like clockwork.

Visually connect.

Talk with fervor.

Be precise about the behavior you appreciate. Models: "I liked the way you asked for a cup of water," or "You worked efficiently obtaining all of your toys."
Offer consideration soon after the behavior you liked. Try not to show consideration soon following a behavior you might have done without. Your youngster needs to have a positive method of acting for something like 30 seconds without the bad way of behaving before you provide them attention.
Offer the type of thoughtfulness your youngster values. If your kid could do without kisses, then, at that point, provide an embrace or a high five all things being equal.
Concentrate totally on even modest improvements. For instance: "That was spectacular tossing your rubbish," or "You made a terrific showing walking into the shop today."
Distinguish methods of behavior that can't happen concurrently. For instance, rather than beating their family, kids may employ

Play-Doh® or communicate carefully as opposed to yelling or weeping.
Nurturing is challenging. All youngsters are distinct and there is no "proper" strategy for nurturing all kids. Nonetheless, there are certain nurturing talents and techniques that will very frequently go far in shaping youngsters' ways of behaving. Around here at The Evidence-Based Practice of Nevada, building nurturing talents is pretty typically a piece of therapy for a youngster. Parent Management Training is a form of therapy that works with guardians in modifying their responses to their kid's style of behaving. The one thing I work with guardians on the most is discovering their kids acting fantastic!

Uplifting comments, approbation, and attention are the most ideal strategies to thoroughly influence behaviour. Taking care of your youngster's perfect methods of behaving can support those ways of behaving with developing in recurrence. As guardians, being engaged with taking care of the unpleasant behaviors is fairly straightforward. "Johnny, leave your sister be. Try not to contact that! Simply plonk down. Quit sobbing." This is ordinary. We as a whole make it happen. What we cannot refute is that for each one (1) revision or "negative" children need to hear five (5) up-sides only to adapt it. A few youngsters require substantially more than that. Youngsters should be discovered to be terrific more (much more) than they should get be "awful."

So how would we make that happen? As a parent, you are likely previously lauding your kids somehow. Continue to do that! Kids generally appreciate this type of praise and you likely feel better offering the appreciation. To employ commendation to construct and encourage an ideal way of behaving, you want to begin by distinguishing what that behavior resembles (for example receiving toys when you ask,

setting the table, supplying to kin, and so on). (for example, getting toys when you ask, preparing the table, offering to kin, and so on.). When you choose the manner of acting, seek to praise that each time it works out. At the point that you applaud, be thrilled and genuine in your tone and face. Likewise, clarify exactly what the youngster performed that is being appreciated, and top it off with a light touch or nonverbal expression of affirmation. Acclaim works greatest on the off chance that it occurs just after the optimal manner of behaving. It might sound something like, "That is fantastic, Suzy! You received your goods promptly when I enquired! Method for going (smile and high five)!"
Methods for discovering kids doing great:

Be sincere and eager

Be specific about the item you are adulating

Add a gentle touch or nonverbal message of endorsement

Give the recognition as close to the perfect method of acting as could realistically be anticipated

Distinguish techniques of acting in advance and subsequently find them fantastic each time you notice

5 to 1 proportion (something else for some youngsters) (something else for certain children)

Do everything it takes not to make it about you (it satisfies me) or about them (you are a decent/miscreant); Make it about the method of acting!

Keep away from underhanded applause "wish you would continually do it along these lines... "

To incorporate more unequivocal recognition in your nurturing, begin by identifying a few ways of behaving you would wish to see more, and thereafter each time they take part in those methods of behaving provide applause. Likewise, give a shot at lauding tiny augmentations. For instance, if you are making superb endeavor labor for one hour on homework, you'll probably need to begin commending more tiny measures of time initially to considerably affect the way of behaving.

Acclaim works for more seasoned youngsters as well. Teens need to hear what they are doing terrific and excess to hear what they are not doing properly. Regardless of whether they overlook the acclaim or offer you an eye-roll, they must hear the commendation, too!

Nurturing is challenging. You are working incredibly hard! You have this!

At the point when we build up our kids' good way of behaving and put out a conscientious endeavor to discover them being fantastic, we'll witness a bigger quantity of this acceptable behavior.

Two Scenarios

Does this sound recognizable? Your kids are enjoying a game together as you straighten up the kitchen after dinner. Unexpectedly, you hear, "Mother, Sarah pushed me!" "Yet, Mom, Sam went ahead!"

Murmuring, you stop cleaning up and stroll into the lounge room to find out the argument before your kids reach boiling point.

Again and again, we ignore the moments our kids are making the greatest option and focus rather on when they are doing some inappropriate behavior. Imagine a situation in which we showed greater gratitude when they made sure to say 'please' and 'thank you without being prompted. Consider the likelihood that we showed thanks toward them for cleaning up their toys purposely.

At the point when we back our kids' positive method of behaving and try to discover them is wonderful, we'll begin to witness substantially a bigger amount of these excellent ways of behaving.

Presently, the image of you are in the kitchen cleaning up and your kids are playing nicely together in the next room. What do you do?

Normally, you endeavor to accomplish so much as might fairly be anticipated while the harmony remains.

Yet, picture a circumstance in which you made it a highlight walk in and let your kids know how amazed you are that they're playing together nicely. Could they perceive you like you're insane?

Kids adore our attentiveness. At the time when they don't obtain it by making the finest decision, they typically turn to some terrible act merely to get a response. We should concentrate on them for the behavior we need to see.

Let's check out the power of good nurturing:

The power of positive nurture may be unexpectedly effective. "Get em being fantastic" has over and again been demonstrated to work on sure behavior in youngsters. While we recognize this is legitimate, the majority of us might likely track down terrible statements to our children the whole day — and the bad remarks may be "merited." As guardians we usually find up rebuking our youngsters with "inspirational" jabbers like:

"I recommended you to get up 10 minutes previous; what's going on with you?"

"How often do I need to counsel you to select your items up from the front room?"

"Which part of 'no' don't you grasp it?"

While these claims might seem like they would encourage you, youngster, to shift, they rarely do. Parental replies like these don't build an atmosphere where your child is permitted to thrive and learn. Truth be told, this technique produces an atmosphere where your youngster could feel scared, despised, and afraid. Furthermore, you are demonstrating behavior you wouldn't feel your youngster should emulate.

Regardless of what your youngsters accomplish, you really must recollect that they are as yet filling in their capacity to regulate contemplations, feelings, and behavior. Your goal, as a parent, is to construct a setting where your kids may over and over attempt to improve and alter unafraid because they understand they are adored, recognized, and valued similarly as they are.

Assuming you believe that your kids should turn into the best version of themselves, you want to zero in on the things they are doing well or can do well. When you distinguish those things, you want to reliably build up your kids for doing these things or endeavoring to do these things.

Ready to check to be positive out? The following are a few ways that might aid you with zeroing down on the item your youngster is doing well (and likely amplify the things they are doing properly too) (and likely increment the things they are doing right too).

Illustrate Who They Are Created to Be
Youngsters rely upon the grown-ups in their world to help them know both what their identity is and who they will be. By depicting

folks you accept they are suited for becoming, you support them by considering this to be doable. At the point when you consider your kids to be skilled, mindful, and able individuals and start letting them know how you envision them becoming these things, you welcome them to become something they may in all probability never have thought about feasible.

Recognize Effort

Mother beaming down at young little girl completing homework

Don't hold on until your kids get it just before you praise them. Search for ways of commending difficult work and exertion rather than essentially applauding results. At the point when you support exertion and assurance, you are both empowering the advancement of these qualities and telling them they are esteemed for who they are instead of just for doing things right. At the point that your kids' endeavors to explore or perform some.

Chapter seven

Make Communication a Priority

You can't anticipate that they should do everything since you, as a parent, "say as much. " They need and merit replies however much grown-ups do. In the event that we don't require some investment to make sense of, youths will start to stress over our convictions and goals and assuming they have any substance. Guardians who reason with their children help them to fathom and learn in a nonjudgmental way.

Make your assumptions understood. On the off chance that there is an issue, examine it, share your considerations, and permit your child to chip away at an answer with you. Be mindful so as to make reference to repercussions. Make thoughts and give options. Be responsive to your kid's suggestions also. Arrange. Kids who participate in decisions are more disposed to complete them.

There are MANY days when I say the initial thing that comes into my viewpoints to my child. "Quit DOING THAT!" Instead of cautiously articulating my requests, "Kindly don't strike your sibling," I holler out directions.

Indeed, you will not be too stunned to even consider finding out, that it doesn't function admirably with my kid.

I made a stride back and acknowledged we don't necessarily in every case effectively speak with another.

You often hear that correspondence is urgent in a marriage. Commonly when there is a correspondence breakdown. There are conflicts, false impressions, and harmed opinions.

As a school clinician, I routinely contemplated points like these. I enjoyed teaching my understudies on the fact that it was so essential to effectively impart our feelings to other people.

Then as a mother, I dynamically lost these essentials. I ended up asking, for what reason isn't my young person paying attention to me while I'm talking?

Of late, I've been thinking about how quickly minutes go and how I need to capitalize on our mid year! I'm trying to claim ignorance our child will be 4 one month from now.

This likewise made me contemplate our correspondence. In addition to the fact that it is essential in marriage, but on the other hand it's critical as a parent!

Why We Should Make Communication With Our Kids a Priority

We want to begin effectively talking with our children today. So when they are teenagers, the roads of contact are as of now open. Beginning contemplating this is rarely too soon!

Presently I would rather not put this colossal load on our shoulders and cause ourselves to feel like we want to get it great or we fizzled!

We learn and advance as guardians. We will not hit the nail on the head always and that is adequate. That is ordinary. Yet, it doesn't mean we can't challenge ourselves and be careful about things as guardians.

I'm focused on protecting an open conversation among myself and my youngsters. I need to figure out how to discuss my opinions with them and help them to talk about their thoughts with me.

Growing up I had a tremendous association with my mother (I actually do!) and I generally regarded how we could let each know other anything. I maintain that should do this with my child and ensure she feels open to offering life to me.

Priorities straight...

To increment correspondence in families investigating present communication is fundamental.

correspondence overview
You might expect you have areas of strength for a culture; at the same time, it's important to stand away and take stock of your genuine association routinely.

Ask yourself how you accept your kids see you,

furthermore...

As a parent, would you say you are measuring up as a powerful communicator?

The following are a couple of individual "Do" inquiries for you to think

In your survey, don't be too serious on yourself since most people have a few regions to develop, including me.

The key is to improve correspondence in families, you should acknowledge your constraints to take a stab at steady development.

Be "absolutely legit" with yourself...

Do you really feel your kids regard you?
Do you accept they see you to be a compatriot?
Do they pay attention to you cautiously and with interest?
Do you accept individuals see you to be a savvy individual?

Do you accept they have confidence in all you say and do?

Do you control your feelings consistently?

Do you pay attention to consideration regarding how your kids are putting themselves out there?

Do you supply them with your whole consideration?

Do you pay attention to appreciate them or basically make an insincere effort as a matter of fact?

Do you show compassion and care for every one of their interests?

Do you advocate the "consolation and backing" of all relatives?

Do you promoter and practice genuineness and regard for all relatives?

Do you impart a sensation of significant worth for your kids' viewpoints and sentiments?

Do you make an opportunity to associate with your kids really?

Also, the Grand-daddy of all...

Do you empower and show" A Positive Attitude" toward everything and everybody consistently?

In the event that you answered "no" to any of the above questions, drive yourself to make a purposeful, genuine, and enthusiastic work to upgrade correspondence in your loved ones.

Make Effective Communication\sa Top Priority

To successfully increment correspondence in families investing significance on our amounts of energy is essential.

Try not to figure you can stand by till your children are more established to start having wonderful, captivating, and invigorating discussions, habitually when they are teenagers it is past the point of no return, they'll have new needs, and associating with Mom and Dad will be tossed on their sideline.

Guardians every now and again accept they are talking appropriately until their youngster unexpectedly suddenly erupts with

Further develop correspondence in your family - The Positive-Parenting Center

"All you at any point do is whine at me"

"You never at any point pay attention to me"

"All I hear is yakkity yak!"

"You don't grasp me"

"You don't have any acquaintance with me"

"You have little to no faith in me"

"You couldn't care less about me".

perhaps most awful yet...

"You don't cherish me".

Remarks of such kind might bushwhack any parent and can be very agonizing. Sadly, it happens far too as often as possible, and to in any case obviously superb families.

Obviously, teenagers are battling with a lot of pressure, vulnerability, and hormonal changes and many elements could prompt such expressions, yet, such disagreeable remarks propose a correspondence issue that should not be messed with

Negative feelings should be dealt with rapidly and never be permitted to putrefy. Warm, caring family culture is tied in with making associations, it demands investment, devotion, and generally fundamental solid "Positive Communication."

Dial back... carve out opportunity to genuinely be aware and comprehend your child, their thought process, their preferences, their number one music, and motion pictures get to know their companions, their desires, dreams, and goals throughout everyday life. Partake in each moment with your youngsters consistently on the grounds that we don't have the foggiest idea what tomorrow might bring.

To really increment correspondence in families, we should shape an early association with our youngsters, kid advancement experts trust that birth to mature fifteen is the central years in fostering the great compatibility that develops into long lasting cheerful and caring associations.

Whatever nurturing stage you are at this moment... "Today" right now is your opportunity to "Resolve to Connect" with your youngsters.

It's so natural to become involved with the high speed universe of bringing up kids, particularly when the two guardians are working (the norm for most families these days) (the standard for most families today).

Great useful correspondence is regularly compromised as "time limitations" have an unexplained approach to overcoming our sincere goals. You should make an opportunity to draw in with your kids day to day truly.

Understanding that "positive nurturing" is tied in with building a charming family climate established on adoration and regard for each other and it is constructed in view of positive and compelling communication is vital."

Here Are...

8 Essential Ways\to\Improve Communication in Families

1) Find Balance in Your Life:

Making time to the interface by finding an equilibrium in your life is by a long shot the most troublesome thing for guardians to do, yet, is perhaps of the most compensating parental accomplishment you can achieve.

The imperatives and time constraints on youthful families these days might overpower, no doubt, and keeping in mind that time itself is estimated, it is subtle and might itself at any point be directed, in any case... you can, and should: "sort out your life around time."

Try to make your "family time" your significant concentration. When you really do this with extraordinary conviction you will see a major significantly impact in your outlook in regards to time and what means quite a bit to you throughout everyday life. Any remaining issues will seem minor and a lot less complex to deal with.

2) Commit to Communicate:

Earnestly promise to convey in a way that you "truly interface" with your kids consistently.

Models:

Focus on customary family feasts (breakfast, lunch, supper) as habitually as conceivable to talk about the day's occasions, for example, what pleasant things happened, or to address any private concerns your youngsters might have. Continuously keep things hopeful.

Go for strolls in the recreation area or around the block after supper or afternoon to consider one-on-one time or as a family together. These times are significant and give opportunities for specific holding time. Indeed, even a five or fifteen-minute walk can offer inestimable benefits.

Set an exceptional family night to play tabletop games, do creates together, or anything that encourages an air ideal for lovely, personal, and holding discourse.

Sleep time is a great opportunity to visit with your little kids, read or make up stories together, and discuss your family or the remarkable things you did as a young person.

As regularly as possible keep the radio off in your drive, this is a fabulous opportunity to make some respectable discussion about any topic of the day.

3) Provide Your Undivided Attention:

At the point when your child converses with you, stop what you're doing, lay out eye to eye connection and listen eagerly to what they need to say consistently.

Assuming you are occupied, never imagine or apathetically pay attention to your child. In the event that you can't pause and offer your total consideration, tell them so and make a guarantee to visit quickly, and make certain to see everything through to completion. This attests their worth to you.

Other than a crisis, do not acknowledge calls or permit different interruptions to defer or upset private visits or novel holding minutes with your kids.

4) Practice Active Listening:

Continuously give your youngster a lot of opportunity to express their considerations and put forth a cognizant attempt to zero in on the words utilized as well as know on non-verbal communication.

Pay attention to fathom their opinions and feelings and deal compassion and understanding for their issues completely.

Recognize their feelings and extend your understanding by repeating how you decipher things in a way that would sound natural to you.

5) Speak at Your Child's Level:

Use terms of your kid's scholarly level to try not to misread your planned message.

Continuously lay out eye to eye connection and in the event that your child is little go directly down to their actual level whenever the situation allows, this disposes of any kind of dread and makes a genuinely necessary sensation of fairness.

Your child paying little mind to progress in years ought to never be constrained or caused to feel docile to you under any condition, they merit equivalent regard.

6) Regulate Your Emotions:

Setting a genuine model here is of essential importance...

Monitor your feelings. Stay cool consistently, particularly when your child shows disagreeable feelings of their own.

Endeavor to remain hopeful while settling contentions and never permit your kid's terrible sentiments to form and incorporate into critical hardships, consistently endeavor toward a mutually beneficial arrangement.

Setting a model for your children is imperative. You can't anticipate that they should get a handle on their own feelings assuming you end up losing your quiet.

7) Encourage Open and Honest Communication:

Continuously support and value genuineness, it is the fundamental base from which all your correspondence is developed. On the off chance that you have no genuineness... point of fact, your relationship will without a doubt come up short.

Your youth has to realize they can put themselves out there sincerely without judgment or contempt for their specific thoughts and values.

Your child will constantly see things from an alternate vantage point than you and regarding their vision and assessment is one of the most essential pieces of lovely and useful family correspondence.

8) Use Positive Communication:

Positive correspondence utilizes more "Do's" than "Don'ts". Tell your kids what you would believe that they should do instead of what not to do.

Try to do you say others should do: recall kids advance as a visual demonstration so don't discuss of others in the event that you don't need your kids to.

Utilize positive empowering remarks consistently and ensure they are certified. Great support is essential in developing completely adjusted youths with positive confidence.

Continuously let your kids in on you have trust in them, reward endeavors not simply results and told them you are consistently glad for them and love them genuinely regardless of what mistakes they make throughout everyday life.

The goal isn't simply to tell them you are pleased with them, at the same time, they ought to continually be incredibly glad for themselves.

Here are only a couple of exceptionally basic models:

What an incredible task you've finished, I'm very satisfied with you.
I have certainty you can achieve anything that you put your energy into.
What an astounding idea you have thought of, decent for you.
What a beautiful comical inclination you have and such an exquisite smile.
What your reasonable decision, you should be very satisfied with yourself.
I can perceive you have enormous trust in yourself, magnificent for you.

That was something great you did, you are a particularly mindful individual

Chapter eight

Show Unconditional love

As a parent, you're responsible for training and coordinating your children. Be that as it may, how you offer your medicinal exhortation has a significant effect on how a young person retains it.

At the point when you need to move toward your child, abstain from denouncing, censuring, or shortcoming findings, which sabotages confidence and may prompt disdain. All things being equal, endeavor to cherish and support, even while reprimanding your children. Ensure they know that while you need and expect better sometime later, your affection is there regardless of anything else.

Unrestricted love is to adore somebody regardless of what life tosses at us.

What is love? As indicated by the book Real Love: The Truth About Finding Unconditional Love and Fulfilling

Relationships,[1] genuine love is genuine love. It is focusing on someone else's pleasure without anticipating any awards for themselves.

It isn't unqualified love when somebody loves you since you can offer them what they want. It is additionally not unrestricted love when somebody simply cherishes you under specific circumstances, similar to when you're cheerful, sound, or wealthy.
Genuine love likewise includes embracing one more person for what their identity is, their defects, and their impediments.

There are circumstances regardless, nobody ought to persevere in an affection relationship.

Unqualified love doesn't suggest "I love you on the off chance that you hurt me."

[2]

Genuine love doesn't suggest you ought to endure very unsafe and noxious demonstrations. At the point when torment comes in more than once, or when the misuse and deceptive nature are involved, responsibility ought to stop.

Genuine love is rarely basic; however, with a tad of work, it's open.
On the off chance that you've never gotten unrestricted love, it can turn out to be difficult to give it out. The following are seven different ways you might rehearse how to adore thusly and change your life.

1. Love isn't how you feel, it is more about how you act.
Attempt to imagine affection as such and you won't go far off-base. If you approach love as a sensation, when you are getting something from another person and afterward you quit getting it then your feelings will modify alongside your direction. An illustration of this is the point

at which you endeavor to be somebody you're not, or perhaps you need to effectively get love: this accordingly has intercourse contingent.

Nonetheless, assuming that you begin to act a specific way and are not requesting another person to be somebody else, then, at that point, that affection is unqualified. Your affection isn't subject to what another person does or says, and that implies you might keep on acting the same way paying little mind to how others act.

At the point when guardians embrace, revere, and show friendship to their youngsters, in any event, when they make mistakes or miss the mark regarding assumptions, this is love unrestricted. All in all, it is a kind of affection without any hidden obligations. In this way, guardians revere their youngsters for what their identity is, regardless of anything else.

Conversely, contingent nurturing furnishes youngsters with the idea that they should procure their folks' fondness. In this manner, young people accept they need to fulfill their folks' assumptions to get their adoration and acknowledgment. As an outcome, such youths will generally show disquiet and keep thinking about whether they are meriting warmth, even after they arrive at development.

Valid, contingent love and tyrant nurturing may bring about unrivaled achievement in youngsters and teens. Be that as it may, the hindering result of contingent love much outperforms these obvious "benefits."

A progression of tests including undergrads found that the individuals who got contingent consent were bound to act how their folks anticipated that they should. In any case, as a result, they would in general despise and severely dislike their folks.

What's more, they normally felt embarrassed or remorseful.

In addition, these specialists likewise dissected ladies who, as youngsters, felt that they were adored just when they satisfied their parent's assumptions. Thusly, they presently felt less meriting as grown-ups, the exploration uncovered. However, regardless of their insight, these ladies were more disposed to use contingent love with their youngsters. Accordingly, the pattern of restrictive love is kept up with.

Love genuine - the force of adoring

The Impact of Loving Unconditionally on the Developing Brain

Many examinations show that horrible parent-youngster bonds at the outset impact mental health.

In particular, a 2012 exploration showed that kids with mindful mothers had a greater hippocampus than people who have been genuinely abused. To make sense, the hippocampus is the region of the mind that oversees memory, learning limit, and responses to push.

"Our review uncovers an undeniable connection between providing care and the size of the hippocampus," said lead scientist Joan L. Luby, MD, teacher of youngster psychiatry. "Having a hippocampus that is more than 10% greater just gives genuine evidence of sustaining's a tremendous impact."

She proceeded, "Guardians ought to be instructed on the most proficient method to support and help their kids. Those are significant fixings in a great turn of events."

The Link Between Emotional Neglect and Disease

Besides, keeping a friendship could have materially influenced all through the outset. For instance, analysts at McGill University in Montreal found that kids who have dictator guardians – guardians who put a lot of consideration on progress and rarely show love – are bound to be fat than youngsters whose guardians continually show friendship. In particular, the exploration on 40,000 youngsters matured 6 to 11 showed that tyrant guardians are 37% bound to create fat children.

Therefore, profound disregard has adverse organic consequences even in adulthood. A 2013 exploration demonstrated that people who had an absence of adoration in the early stages were more worried and had expanded disease risk.

Specialists assessed individuals who persevered through profound or actual abuse as a youngster, with next to zero parental love and sympathy. As an outcome, researchers uncovered that these individuals had a remarkably elevated risk for sickness across every substantial framework.

Notwithstanding, the investigation additionally discovered that parental warmth and friendship safeguard kids against the unsafe natural effect of young life stress. In addition, fondness brought down the frequency of grown-up sickness. Accordingly, the advantage of unqualified love on actual well-being is undeniable.

solid associations

Genuine Love Builds a Foundation for Healthy Relationships

One more exploration on parent-kid collaborations demonstrated that ladies who were less controlling while at the same time playing with their small kids had more noteworthy binds with their children.

Thusly, scientists accepted that the youngsters with less-controlling mothers felt more acknowledged and adored — prompting better connections.

Subsequently, genuine love impacts the parent-kid connection interface. Besides, this connection influences a kid's ability to foster genuine bonds. Moreover, it influences how effectively that young person will want to fabricate significant connections as a teen and a grown-up.

Youngsters or teens with a steady association realize that their folks are sincerely present and receptive to dealing with them. In this manner, they figure out how to trust and depend on others. Moreover, they are better ready to deal with their feelings and be their genuine selves.

Thus, this empowers a genuine relationship. In any case, they will more often than not feel uncomfortable, stressed, and apprehensive. This prompts ways of behaving going from forceful and requesting to sticking and dependant.

companionship and love

Genuine Love and the Brain's Reward System

Also, one exploration has pinpointed the pieces of the mind that took part in this kind of affection. Scientists at Montreal University encouraged members to feel fondness for specific people in a succession of photographs. At the same time, they filtered their cerebrums utilizing an fMRI scanner.

As a result, they confirmed that this kind of adoration remembers an alternate brain network for the cerebrum. In particular, seven locales of the cerebrum are connected with this inclination. Besides, this organization envelops cerebrum regions that are additionally participated in heartfelt and maternal love.

In addition, a few of these designs are basic parts of the mind's prize framework. All in all, a portion of the districts animated when an individual offers love genuinely are likewise engaged with producing dopamine, the synthetic engaged with seeing joy.

"The compensating normal for genuine love supports the foundation of profound close-to-home ties. Such strong ties may significantly add to the endurance of the human species."

—Teacher Mario Beauregard, a fundamental specialist for the Montreal University study

Empathy, Meditation, and Unconditional Love

Empathy is an essential element of genuine love. Furthermore, we can reinforce our "sympathy muscle." Specifically, reflection has been shown to support our capacity for encountering empathy and love. Besides, a strategy known as cherishing benevolence contemplation (LKM) has been shown to advance both of these sentiments.

Positive brain science specialist Barbara Fredrickson investigated the impact of LKM on feelings and making individual assets. Members practiced LKM consistently for a considerable length of time. Consequently, specialists analyzed the progressions in their encounters with blissful feelings, their resistance to affliction, and their connections with others.

As per Fredrickson, "The act of LKM prompted modifications in individuals' ordinary encounters of an expansive assortment of positive sentiments, including love, joy, appreciation, happiness, good faith, pride, interest, entertainment, and wonder."

Also, another examination analyzed the minds of the individuals who had rehearsed LKM for somewhere around 10,000 hours with individuals who were new to contemplation. As a result, specialists saw that LKM meditators showed higher action in the insula and the fleeting parietal intersection, two regions of the cerebrum critical for the ability to identify.

Moreover, specialists at Stanford University found that main seven minutes of LKM upgraded members' view of social connectedness with others. "These discoveries suggest that this promptly applied procedure might help to support lovely social sentiments and reduce social disengagement," the exploration creators finished up.

Coordinating Self Love

Grown-ups who didn't get love genuinely as kids are in many cases extremely severe with themselves. At the end of the day, they don't feel meriting cherishing. Along these lines, they find it hard to excuse themselves for their deficiencies and to acknowledge themselves as they are.

Nonetheless, the act of self-sympathy might assist with recuperating the connection injury that happens from contingent love. Research on self-empathy recommends that it enjoys a few valuable benefits, including

Expanded satisfaction
More noteworthy hopefulness
More energetic temperament
Diminished pressure
More grounded individual drive
A sensation of interest and investigation
Suitability
Good faith
Better ability to associate with individuals.
Besides, self-sympathy is a more strong inspiration than confidence, as indicated by scientist Kristin Neff. In particular, confidence depends on our triumphs and others' impressions of us. Nonetheless, self-empathy involves a tireless demeanor of acknowledgment and graciousness toward ourselves — as such, unqualified confidence.

To reiterate, youngsters who get genuine love from their folks have higher pressure opposition, better wellbeing, more grounded confidence, and better mental health. Along these lines, it is indispensable for good close to home and actual turn of events.

All in all, people, everything being equal, may improve their ability to offer themselves as well as other people love – by rehearsing empathy and self-sympathy, on Mother's Day and consistently.

Chapter nine

TRY NOT TO SPANK, NO MATTER WHAT

It's time for parents to forsake the old cliché that youngsters "deserve a good spanking" every once in a while.

The American Academy of Pediatrics (AAP) released a forceful statement in 2018, encouraging parents not to spank their children, based on a growing pile of research demonstrating that the disciplinary practice causes more damage than good.

"The new AAP statement includes data that show that kids who were spanked in their early years were more likely to be more defiant, show more aggressive behavior later in preschool and school, and have increased risk for mental health disorders and lower self-esteem," says pediatrician Karen Estrella, MD.

Research over the past 20 years has proven that slapping increases hostility in young children and is unsuccessful in modifying their unwanted conduct, the AAP states. Studies have also connected spanking to an increased risk of mental health issues and decreased brain development.

The AAP is a prominent professional organization that represents roughly 67,000 doctors throughout the nation. But this development in thinking about parental discipline isn't simply restricted to medical professionals – fewer parents raising children now appear to embrace spanking. In a 2013 survey, almost half of parents under the age of 36 admitted having spanked their children. Among all of the elder generations, that figure was 70% or higher.

Why spanking to discipline doesn't work
While spanking may instill a feeling of terror in your kid at the moment, it won't enhance conduct over the long run. In reality, consistent spanking normalizes the act of striking and may lead to aggressive behavior that invites prolonged conflict between you and your kid.

"Children consider their parents as role models," Dr. Estrella explains. "Aggressive conduct will simply develop more bad behaviors in a child."

In their statement, the AAP also criticized verbal abuse, adding that screaming in a manner that insults, humiliates, or shames a child also has harmful consequences on brain development.

"Research demonstrates that youngsters exposed to toxic stress have abnormalities in their cognitive skills later on," Dr. Estrella explains.

Discipline ideas to utilize instead of spanking
Try these three ways to properly punish your child:

Establish a pleasant and supportive parent-child connection that offers your youngster an incentive to display excellent conduct.
Use positive reinforcement to urge your youngster to behave.
If necessary, utilize alternative disciplinary tactics such as time-outs or taking away your child's favorite privileges for some time.
Dr. Estrella adds on those and other suggestions from the AAP with these additional tips:

Be a role model. Make it a point to stay cool, with the idea that your kid looks to you to be an example of how to act.
Set guidelines and boundaries that can be enforced uniformly among all caregivers. There should be no good man/bad guy for your kid with numerous providers.
Make sure that regulations are verbalized using age-appropriate terminology.
Constantly praise and applaud favorable behavior. Give attention to actions that you want your youngster to repeat. Show that you are watchful and pleased when they act nicely.
Similarly, know when not to answer. "Ignoring a harmful behavior, for example, if a youngster throws himself to the floor because he wasn't permitted to play on the iPad, is a smart strategy to help that behavior

diminishes over time," Dr. Estrella explains. "In this situation, the youngster will learn that throwing a tantrum will not bring him the iPad."

Learn from prior experience. What prompts your child's misbehavior? If you can identify a trigger, are there methods to prevent it, or at least better prepare for it? Make sure your kid understands what the repercussions will be if they don't comply with your wishes or misbehaves in a given setting.

Redirect negative conduct. Turn "don't do that" into an activity that your youngster can undertake. If your kid grabs a toy from a playmate, for example, give your child another toy or activity until it's their time. Use the same approach for winning/losing scenarios.

Call a time out when a rule is breached. Remove your kid from that setting for a pre-set duration of time, which may be one minute each year of age. Explain in a brief statement why you are doing it. Once your kid becomes older, let them lead the time out by stating, "Go to time out and come back when you are calm and ready.

A growing body of studies has revealed that spanking and other types of physical punishment may pose substantial hazards to children, but many parents aren't getting the message.

"It's a very controversial area even though the research is extremely telling and very clear and consistent about the negative effects on children," says Sandra Graham-Bermann, Ph.D., a psychology professor and principal investigator for the Child Violence and Trauma

Laboratory at the University of Michigan. “People become irritated and strike their kids. Maybe they don’t realize there are other options.”

Many studies have indicated that physical punishment — including spanking, punching, and other techniques of producing pain — may lead to increased aggressiveness, antisocial behavior, physical harm, and mental health issues for children. Americans’ approval of physical punishment has fallen since the 1960s, although studies indicate that two-thirds of Americans still approve of parents slapping their kids.

But slapping doesn’t work, says Alan Kazdin, Ph.D., a Yale University psychology professor and head of the Yale Parenting Center and Child Conduct Clinic. “You cannot punish out these habits that you do not want,” adds Kazdin, who served as APA president in 2008. “There is no necessity for physical punishment based on the findings. We are not giving up an efficient method. We are saying this is a dreadful thing that does not work.”

Evidence of damage

On the international stage, physical punishment is increasingly being considered a breach of children’s human rights. The United Nations Committee on the Rights of the Child published a directive in 2006 declaring physical punishment “legalized violence against children” that should be eradicated in all contexts by “legislative, administrative, social and pedagogical measures." The treaty that formed the committee has been backed by 192 nations, with only the United States and Somalia declining to ratify it.

Around the globe, 30 nations have prohibited the physical punishment of children in all situations, including the home. The legislative restrictions normally have been utilized as public education tools, rather than efforts to criminalize conduct by parents who spank their children, says Elizabeth Gershoff, Ph.D., a major researcher on physical punishment at the University of Texas at Austin.

"Physical punishment doesn't work to encourage kids to cooperate, so parents assume they have to keep intensifying it. That is why it is so dangerous," she explains.

After evaluating decades of research, Gershoff prepared the Report on Physical Punishment in the United States: What Research Tells Us About Its Effects on Children, released in 2008 in partnership with Phoenix Children's Hospital. The research suggests that parents and caregivers make every effort to avoid physical punishment and argues for the outlawing of physical discipline in all U.S. schools. The study has been approved by dozens of organizations, including the American Academy of Pediatrics, the American Medical Association, and Psychologists for Social Responsibility.

After three years of work on the APA Task Force on Physical Punishment of Children, Gershoff and Graham-Bermann issued a report in 2008 detailing the task force's recommendations. That research suggests that "parents and caregivers decrease and perhaps eliminate their use of any physical punishment as a discipline method." The study calls on psychologists and other specialists to "indicate to parents that physical punishment is not a suitable, or even a consistently successful, means of discipline."

"We have the potential here to take a bold statement in favor of safeguarding children," says Graham-Bermann, who led the task committee.

APA's Committee on Children, Youth and Families (CYF) and the Board for the Advancement of Psychology in the Public Interest unanimously endorsed a proposed resolution last year based on the task force recommendations. It adds that APA supports "parents' use of non-physical ways of disciplining children" and condemns "the use of harsh or damaging physical punishment of any child." APA also should fund more research and a public education campaign on "the efficacy and results associated with corporal punishment and nonphysical means of discipline," the draft resolution adds. After gathering input from other APA boards and committees in the spring of 2012, APA's Council of Representatives will consider adopting the resolution as APA policy.

Preston Britner, Ph.D., a child developmental psychologist, and professor at the University of Connecticut, helped prepare the proposed resolution as co-chair of CYF. "It covers the concerns about physical punishment and a growing corpus of research on alternatives to physical punishment, along with the premise that psychology and psychologists have much to offer to the development of those other strategies," he adds.

More than three decades have passed since APA endorsed a resolution in 1975 banning corporal punishment in schools and other institutions, but it didn't address physical discipline in the family. That resolution said that physical punishment might "instill hatred, resentment and a feeling of helplessness without lessening the unwanted behavior."

Research findings

Physical punishment may work briefly to halt harmful conduct because children are terrified of being struck, but it doesn't work in the long term and can make youngsters more aggressive, Graham-Bermann adds.

Research published last year in Child Abuse and Neglect indicated an intergenerational cycle of violence in families where physical punishment was utilized. Researchers questioned parents and children aged 3 to 7 from more than 100 homes. Children who were physically disciplined were more likely to accept striking as a strategy for settling their problems with classmates and siblings. Parents who had undergone regular physical punishment during their youth were more likely to feel it was appropriate, and they often spanked their children. Their children, in turn, frequently felt spanking was an acceptable discipline strategy.

The detrimental impacts of physical punishment may not become obvious for some time, Gershoff explains. "A youngster doesn't get slapped and then rush out and steal a store," she explains. "There are indirect changes in how the youngster thinks about things and feels about them."

As in many fields of science, some experts differ regarding the validity of the studies on corporal punishment. Robert Larzelere, Ph.D., an Oklahoma State University professor who studies parental discipline, was a member of the APA task group who published his minority report because he disagreed with the scientific foundation of the task force recommendations. While he thinks that parents should decrease their use of physical punishment, he says most of the referenced studies are correlational and don't indicate a direct relationship between physical punishment and long-term bad impacts on children.

"The findings do not differentiate effectively between non-abusive and unduly harsh methods of physical punishment," Larzelere explains. "You obtain poorer results from physical punishment than from other disciplinary approaches only when it is utilized more harshly or as the principal discipline tactic."

In a meta-analysis of 26 studies, Larzelere and a colleague found that an approach they described as "conditional spanking" led to greater reductions in child defiance or anti-social behavior than 10 of 13 alternative discipline techniques, including reasoning, removal of privileges, and time out (Clinical Child and Family Psychology Review, 2005). (Clinical Child and Family Psychology Review, 2005). Larzelere describes conditional spanking as a disciplinary approach for 2- to 6-year-old children in which parents employ two open-handed swats on the buttocks only after the kid has refused softer treatment such as time out.

Gershoff believes all of the research on physical punishment have certain limitations. "Unfortunately, any study on parent discipline is going to be correlational since we can't randomly assign kids to parents for an experiment. But I don't believe we have to ignore every study that has been done," she argues. "I can just about count on one hand the studies that have shown anything beneficial regarding physical punishment and hundreds that have been negative."

Teaching new skills

If parents aren't allowed to smack their kids, what nonviolent tactics can aid with discipline? The Parent Management Training program directed by Kazdin at Yale is founded upon research on applied behavioral analysis. The program encourages parents to utilize positive reinforcement and effusive praise to reward children for excellent conduct.

Kazdin also utilizes a tactic that may seem like craziness to most parents: Telling children to practice throwing a tantrum. Parents advise their children to conduct a simulated tantrum without one undesired feature, such as hitting or kicking. Gradually, when youngsters learn to regulate tantrums when they aren't furious, their true tantrums reduce, Kazdin adds.

Remaining cool throughout a child's tantrums is the best method, paired with time-outs when required and a regular disciplinary plan that promotes good conduct,

Chapter ten

Adapt your parenting to fit your child.

Children are typically considered as the result of their surroundings and their parents' child-raising abilities. While kids are strongly impacted by their familial surroundings, they arrive into the world with extremely diverse personalities and attributes. Parents frequently realize that tactics that work with one kid may not work as well with another. Bringing up children is a "two-way street" in which parents and children both participate. This article presents an overview of data on the relevance of synchrony between parenting approaches and child features and explains ways in which parenting may be adapted to "fit" the kid.

Temperament researchers such as Rothbart and Bates (2006) highlight the large differences that exist between children on qualities such as reactivity - the intensity or mildness with which a child acts and reacts; sociability - how at ease a child is when meeting new people or in new situations; and self-regulation - a child's ability to control his/her attention, emotions and behavior. More particular temperament features (e.g. sensitivity, activity) are also commonly recognized, however, they may be considered as parts of the three broad aspects just mentioned. Each kid has a particular blend of temperament characteristics and they constitute part of his/her intrinsic make-up. Children's temperament qualities are obvious from birth and considered to be biologically rooted, but they may be modified to some degree by the child's subsequent experiences.

A substantial body of research suggests that a child's temperament type correlates to his/her welfare (see the review by Sanson, Hemphill, & Smart 2004). (see the review by Sanson, Hemphill, & Smart 2004). For example, shyness and/or high reactivity have been identified to be risk factors for anxiety; and high reactivity and/or poor self-regulation (particularly of emotions but also of attention) are associated with the development of externalizing disorders such as violence and oppositional behavior. On the other hand, temperament features such as strong self-control and a calm, easygoing attitude (i.e. low reactivity) are connected with the development of good social skills and prosocial capabilities such as empathy. A kid's temperament type may also impact other people's responses to the youngster. For example, an adaptable, confident youngster is often easier to deal with than an intense, timid one, which may offer up more options for the sunny-natured child. These personality variations might drive the youngster to seek out places in which he/she feels comfortable (termed "niche selection" by Scarr & McCartney, 1983), possibly reducing the child's range of experiences. Thus, a child's temperament style can exert a large influence on his/her development, and can also affect parent-child relationships and family life.

Connections between parenting and child wellbeing

Certain aspects of parenting are known to benefit all children. For example, a warm and supportive parent-child connection is viewed as the cornerstone of good parenting (Dishion & McMahon, 1998). (Dishion & McMahon, 1998). Supervision of children's activities and friendships (commonly dubbed "monitoring"), especially in the teenage years, seems of major significance and its absence is associated with a variety of negative outcomes, such as adolescent antisocial conduct and drug use (e.g. Barnes & Farrell, 1992). (e.g. Barnes & Farrell, 1992). Limit setting and consistency are fundamental components of "authoritative" parenting (Baumrind, 1989), which is commonly viewed as the most optimum kind of parenting. Conversely, harsh or over-controlling parenting practices are linked to the development of behavior disorders in childhood and adolescence (e.g. Bender, Allen, & McElhaney, 2007). (e.g. Bender, Allen, & McElhaney, 2007).

However, there is compelling evidence that competent parenting is more vital for certain children than others. Research from the Australian Temperament Project (ATP) indicated that rates of issues were substantially greater.

Social skills were best among the first group, slightly lower among the second and third groups, and lowest among the group with both kinds of issues (see Figure 2). (see Figure 2). These results highlight the larger risk for issues among disadvantaged children if there are challenges in the parent-child interaction. Encouragingly, studies also imply that most parents find means of controlling their children and building excellent connections with them, even when their kid is more challenging than average in temperament type.

Within the broad limits of successful parenting is the emerging realization that "one size does not fit all" - that certain parenting practices mesh well with specific sorts of children while other approaches work less effectively. Two categories of children have been the center of attention; firstly, timid, scared, reticent youngsters; and secondly, those that are explosive, combative, and hard to handle.

Research results about the parenting of timid, hesitant youngsters

Shy, fearful children have been described as "slow to warm up" (Thomas & Chess, 1977). (Thomas & Chess, 1977). They tend to be cautious, and prefer to wait and see. They adjust more slowly to novelty and change than other youngsters, but once they feel at home may be social, friendly, and adventurous. The research undertaken by Graznya Kochanska (1997) showed that the conscience development of shy, reticent children was facilitated by a gentle style of discipline characterized by encouragement rather than threats. Such parenting was less beneficial for fearless children, for whom the application of consequences and a strong parent-child bond were more significant for conscience development.

Similarly, Rubin, Cheah, & Fox (2001) showed that over-protective parenting, in which children's exposure to stressful events is restricted or regulated by an adult, was particularly damaging for timid, hesitant youngsters. Over-protection may limit a child's range of social experiences and impede the child from learning how to manage stress and gain a sense of mastery from doing so. Rubin's and colleagues' study revealed that when shy youngsters were over-protected, the risk of internalizing difficulties (e.g. anxiety, dissatisfaction) dramatically rose. However, parental over-protection did not seem to have such effects on more sociable, outgoing children. This study team also showed that timid reticent youngsters prospered when parental direction and support were strong.

Together, these data show that a gentle, encouraging parenting strategy, which gives direction and support without tipping over into over-protection and control, is especially useful for timid, reticent, or scared children.

Research results about the parenting of explosive, feisty youngsters

Children who are volatile and feisty can be challenging to parent. They respond intensely and strongly, can be easily frustrated, and find it hard to control their emotions. Parents' boundaries and regulations may be questioned, and parents may feel their resolve eroded or react more aggressively in an attempt to keep control. Gerald Patterson and colleagues describe this as a "coercive cycle" (Patterson, Reid, & Dishion, 1992;

Scaramella & Leve, 2004). (Patterson, Reid, & Dishion, 1992; Scaramella & Leve, 2004). Patterson's hypothesis claims that inexperienced or less competent parents, who may overreact to little non-compliance, are rigid, or employ harsh or inconsistent punishment, are prone to get engaged in unpleasant relationships with temperamentally volatile children. These intensify over time as parents and children raise their demands on each other and frequently culminate with the parent resorting to physical punishment or giving up. The youngster learns that demanding conduct may be effective, aggressiveness is acceptable, and fails to acquire alternative problem-solving methods.
Aggressive behaviors may then become engrained over time, resulting in peer rejection, academic failure, attachment to antisocial companions, and antisocial behavior in adolescence. There is abundant evidence supporting many elements of this notion.
Drawing from this study, parenting that is aggressive, patient, and tough as well as warm and loving looks most suited for volatile, feisty children. A soft style of parenting is less successful with these youngsters. Limit setting, maintaining consistency, and following through with penalties are equally vital, as are parental support and affirmation of positive conduct (e.g. praising, rewarding) (e.g. praising, rewarding). Finally, the data is clear-cut concerning the long-term harmful consequences of harsh or physical punishment on these children.

Translating the results into practice

How, therefore, may parenting be altered to harmonize with kid characteristics? Some advice for parents and practitioners is offered below, as well as a description of some effective temperament-focused parenting approaches and relevant resources.

Firstly, it is crucial for parents and experts to grasp that a child's temperament type is neither "excellent" nor "bad" on its own, but very much dependent on the context and scenario. For example, a home with a wide garden may better fit a very active child's energetic manner than a compact apartment, and high activity may encroach less on family life under the former conditions. The "fit" between the child's temperament type and his/her surroundings is vital.

Hence, parents should be encouraged to appreciate their child's positive qualities, strengths, and the things he/she does well, or as McClowry suggests, "affirm the child's goodness and talents" (p. 63). (p. 63). Likewise, it is crucial to recognize the child's temperament type and appreciate the child's individuality without comparing him/her to other children or attempting to recreate his/her core disposition. By knowing the kid's temperament, parents may work with, rather than against, the youngster. Labeling the kid as "easy" or "difficult" must be avoided, since this may become self-fulfilling and restrictive. Research shows that some change in children's temperament style normally occurs as they grow up, acquire new skills, and expand their capacities (see Sanson, Letcher, & Smart, 2007). (see Sanson, Letcher, & Smart, 2007).

How can we help parents gain an understanding of their child's temperament? There are at least two possibilities here: a) seek parents' observations of their child's typical style over time, and b) invite parents to complete temperament-focused questions. Each can then be used as a basis for dialogue about the child's temperamental tendencies and ways of working with these. McClowry (2003) advises that parents be supplied with an overview on the nature of child temperament, and then encouraged to maintain a record over several days of how their kid handles unexpected changes in activities or stressful events. Some likely scenarios are when the child has to stop doing an enjoyable activity (e.g. watching television), when there is a change in plans (e.g. a delay or abandonment of an outing), or when the child is asked to follow an instruction (e.g. change clothes) (e.g. change clothes). Parents should pay attention to how the child reacts (e.g. mildly or strongly, happily or unhappily) rather than what he/she does, noting aspects such as how prolonged the child's reaction is, and the intensity with which he/she reacts. From this, a picture of the child's normal style should emerge.

It can also be helpful for parents to complete a temperament questionnaire about their child.

www.ingramcontent.com/pod-product-compliance
Lightning Source LLC
La Vergne TN
LVHW010610160826
845677LV00013B/3348
9798848198607